TO MY

ANGEL

IN THE

SKY

To My Angel in the Sky

A collection of poems
and letters

By Alexa Suarez U.

Disclaimer

This book does not replace the advice of a medical professional. The reader should consult a physician in matters relating to his/her physical and mental health and particularly with respect to any symptoms that may require diagnosis or medical attention. Please seek mental and physical health from a professional when necessary. Although the author has made every effort to ensure that the information in this book was correct at press time, the author does not assume and hereby disclaims any liability to any party for any loss, damage, or disruption caused by errors or omissions, whether such errors or omissions result from negligence, accident, or any other cause. Keep in mind the details and experiences are written by the author's perspective. To maintain the anonymity of the individuals involved, there have been change in some details.

A special thanks to my supporters,

especially my biggest supporter, you dad.

Table of Contents

To My Angel in the Sky

It's been a week and one day since you left earth.

The pain doesn't get easier,

I find myself thinking about you every second my mind is not

occupied.

Sometimes I think that you'll walk through my bedroom door with

a big smile on your face and your tail wagging.

What's worse is that, because I think about you all the time, I keep

trying to call you or mention your name. It's not only until the

words leave my mouth,

That I realize that you are no longer here.

The worst part of it all is the sleepless nights.

Every time I blink or close my eyes to have peace of mind, I see you

having the seizure all over again.

I see your body shaking and moving horrifically.

I

My mind still echoes the cries I made as I beg you to stay with me,

I cry out your name over and over, but your body does not
improve. It wasn't until several minutes passed that it finally
stopped.

I wish it was all just a nightmare,
Even now I still expect myself to wake up and have you next to me
like it was all just a dream,
As if it never happened.
Other days I feel almost nothing.

I have grown stronger, yet I have my days where I am completely
defenseless,
Beaten by my thoughts.
Sometimes I even wondered if I had made the right decision,
I think back to how you were after the seizure and realize how
much it hurt us all even more.

My eyes continue to produce tears like a rainforest,

On and off.

Despite what has happened I must leave it aside,

Because "life moves on" and is something I must do for your sake

and mine.

I miss you,

I wish I could be with you in heaven.

Alas, I cannot for you would not want me to go so soon,

I'll keep that promise to my dying days.

Love, Alexa.

The Day You Were Gone

At first, I felt nothing.

My brain, my heart, and my body didn't know how to feel.

"Was it due to shock?"

"Am I not registering this?"

"Have I lost my mind ?" I would ask myself.

It all happens so quickly and much too soon.

One minute you were in my arms,

The next minute all I can do is hold myself.

I sat there against the wall trying to comprehend it all.

Completely loss of words

Wondering where it had all gone wrong.

I promised you I would stay

But all I want to do is see you.

You were right there.

I replay the scene back in my mind recalling what the vet had told

me.

The paperwork,

The procedure,

The despair.

I can still recall every detail,

How the room smelt like,

The faces of the vets,

And your facial expression.

All this weight I had carried on my shoulders.

I wish I had other options,

One where you weren't struggling.

And one where I didn't have to make the choice.

Funny how this all happened hours ago,

Yet it feels like seconds have passed.

A Talk with the Grim Reaper

He stood there,

          In silence above your body

          And next to mine.

          We don't say a word,

          For silence spoke for me.

          He holds you with one hand.

          Leaving with your last breath.

          I crumble under my knees.

"Was there something I could've done to make it better?" I

          whispered to myself.

          He returns without you by his side

          And held my hand in return.

          His touch was the real surprise,

          A sense of warmness and comfort.

          "He's at peace now" he reassures me.

          Knowing it would give me *some* relief.

          "I know" is all I can muster.

          He wipes a tear off my cheek.

Analyzing it delicately.

"Does it ever get easier?"

"Death?"

"No, life."

"Only time will tell."

The Internal I

When you had left, everything suddenly turned dark. I became lost. I sat outside in the grass listening to the voices all around. The sun had set, and I had not moved. I don't know how I ended up here and part of me didn't feel like leaving. Over time a shower of rain had turned into a storm. I stood there surrounded by a forest that I had not known. I had lost it all. My mind is completely insane. The thunder roared like the wrath of Zeus himself. My spirits are slaughtered by a clean scythe. My body was heavy, and my clothes were completely soaked, but I refused to move. I screamed at the universe with all my might, not caring about the consequences that might follow, "nothing can be worse than this" I would think. Trees swayed side by side almost as if they were waving me away. Leaves brushing against my skin as the wind took them away. "Run" they would squeal. Right out of the sky, a lightning bolt strikes, and my vision closes in. Electricity runs through my veins, a burning sensation of a thousand needles. I scream in agony.

Weeds and Flowers

Every flower

Withers.

Whether or not it has been

Plucked,

Will define its fate.

Some Words Cannot Explain the Feeling

I close the door behind me,

Blocking everything out,

Weighing myself down.

No one says a word to me,

Not a whisper

Nor a glance.

Absolutely nothing.

Is it nothing?

Is it pain?

Numbness.

Both at the same time yet neither.

When they're gone,

I

Allow

Myself to

Feel.

It hurts

Burns

And breaks.

I lay down on the ground.

I stare above

Letting the melody of the storm speak for me.

If only...

I feel so hopeless.

Not because there is nothing more I can do,

Not because of the work stacked against

The walls,

Not because of the obstacles Life brings.

It is everything.

The Next Day

I open my eyes for a new day.

My mind suppresses the idea of yesterday.

Yesterday.

How could I ever forget?

I pull away from my bedsheets with the cold greeting me,

It welcomes me.

The creaks of the wooden floor shout every step I take.

I slowly leave the room.

My eyes are still completely swollen. I take a deep breath.

An ache in my chest follows.

In the background, my alarm makes the slightest noise,

enough for me to move an inch.

"Maybe it was all a dream?" Denial tells me.

I change and prepare for a new day of work.

Glancing back at the mirror glimmered a speck of hope.

Hope for a new day.

I entered the hallway where you had once slept.

The bed was gone.

You were gone.

My hope was gone.

9/17

Dear my sweet little angel,

I saw you in my dream, I feel awful, I felt like I should've given you more time. I keep blaming myself, but I also need to remember that you were suffering too.

I was so relieved at the thought that you were alive, by the time I woke up, reality just crashed down on me. I miss you.

I tried my best to pull myself together. I couldn't help but lose myself when I saw your ashes and the certificate.

It broke me.

If only I knew how you felt right now.

Someday I'll join you. But for now, I will live for the both of us.

Questions

"How old is he ?"

They would ask as you stood before me.

"Wow that's old"

They say after.

Now they don't ask at all.

Another Goes, an Hour, Minute, and Era

Each moment that passes only feeds into my longing.

It's almost as if Time were to be the villain as I spend my days,

Weeks,

Months,

Possibly centuries,

Waiting for the day we meet again.

Waiting for time to pass,

Is torture,

Empty,

And completely destructive.

I continue to live for it was your last wish.

I live for both of us.

I live because you gave me that purpose.

I still believe everything is just a dream.

Denial is a feeling I cannot escape.

Time is all that it takes to heal,

At least that's what they say.

Seclusion Among the Shell

When you're gone,

Like a turtle, I went back inside my shell.

Secluding myself from the outside world and into what is left of

my imagination.

Gone to the old ways before I met you.

Locking up my heart and soul,

Moving in an empty ~~corpse~~ body.

Living as an entity where I can longer get

Harmed.

Me, myself, and I.

The three protectors left.

Losing you reminded me of how much was at risk.

Without you, these walls I have built are all I can lean on.

More and More

As the day goes on, I pray that it will be hectic,

Where my work is stacked over and over again

Until my mind is focused on the tasks.

I try to keep myself busy because when I don't,

It hurts.

My mind shifts into a weapon

And my heart it's enemy.

In response, I add to the stress.

More paperwork.

More chores.

More courses.

More to do.

My mind is busy and stressed but at least it's not depressed.

My lungs begging for a breath,

My bones quiver in each movement,

My veins pulsing every second,

And my heart is stone cold.

All to put my problems away.

And Then It Went Dark

Who would've known that the moments

I thought were supposed to be happy,

Had turned so quickly into a *tragedy*.

The popsicle begins to melt away,

Leaving a dull,

Brittle,

Stained stick.

Happy Birthday: A Wish of You

In front of me stands colorful candles on top of a chocolate cake.

My favorite type of cake.

I stare at them and glance around the room.

Instinctively my arm reaches under the table.

They sing and clap with cheer,

How can they be doing this? You were gone for only 2 weeks.

Yet here I am playing the fool,

My hand grasps the air.

You were supposed to be here.

I smile at them feeding into their satisfaction.

When the song ended, I knew what was coming.

"Make a wish!"

I know it will never come true.

I close my eyes and blow.

I open them and look around.

They clap their hands and cheer.

A sigh escapes from my lips.

I bring my arm back and take a slice. Gazing at the burnt candles.

When it is all over,

I am thankful

—Thankful that I do not need to continue this.

If only my wish came true, I think to myself.

I close my eyes imagining you with your wings,

Sitting next to me in spirit, the whole time.

The One at Night

As the time goes on and the night comes and sweeps you under

your feet

You surround yourself with warmth.

Blankets and pillows scattered everywhere,

Nothing seems to work.

I close my eyes and I try not to see you.

At least not in the way you were that day.

Memories flood out of my pillow and into my head.

I turn to the other side,

Restless for sleep to come.

Where oh where did the Sandman go when I needed him most?

I open my eyes before Nightmare comes towards me.

He disguises himself as you.

I should be happy and relieved.

But the scene changes and I see you disappear once again.

Gone like the sand slipping through my fingers.

I shift back facing the ceiling with my hands by my side and my

eyes open.

A sigh of frustration escapes my lips.

"You should be sleeping," he whispers.

10/9

Dear my sweet little angel,

It has been a little over a month since you left, yet it doesn't feel like that. There are so many nights that I have yearned to see you. I miss holding on to you when I am stressed, happy, sad, all the highs, and all the lows. I miss everything. One minute I'll be fine, and the next I am completely torn as soon as I am reminded of you having a seizure. "It's all in your head," I tell myself as I try to shake away the image. It feels engraved in my head and plays like a film over and over. To make it all go away I listen to songs that bring out the best memories of you.

There are moments when I look at the time, I think of our routine. The times I would give you breakfast, lunch, dinner, and treats that followed. Instinctively I keep those thoughts at bay as I can. I try not to let them

overpower me or become intrusive but rather remind

myself of all the light that you had shone in the darkness,

which will never go in vain.

Your Song

Listening to music felt like therapy.

The melody and the words express everything I couldn't.

Each line is as impactful as the next. Almost as if it fed into my life

support.

In the back of my mind, I can almost hear your voice.

Almost,

Had it not been for my imagination.

When You are Not Here

"Where did they go?"
"What happened?"
I ask myself every day.

How quickly life happens right before your eyes.
One second, they're there,
The next they're gone.

I used to think that I was never alone,
But now I laugh at that thought.

Don't get me wrong I always loved being alone.
Accepting the comfort of my solitude.
But I despise feeling alone in a crowded room.

The feeling sets in slowly like venom
Only for you to see it after it is too late.
With it follows yearning and self-hatred.

I miss you.
My sweet companion, friend, and family.

You made the hard days bearable and the happiest day happier.

With you, loneliness was never a word.

Now loneliness is all I feel.

My Support System

"Come on smile,

Show those perfect porcelain teeth" They would say.

The screen lightens.

"How are you?" They would text.

"Well, it's been hard since he passed." I would respond honestly.

No text back.

Then the crash came.

"Hey!" Message sent the next day.

No text back.

So I walked away to the rest. The ones that care.

The screen flashes again but this time with meaning from someone

who has been there.

34

Someone whose heart is full of gold.

"Hey. I'm here if you need me." Understanding my sadness eye to

eye.

"Thank you. I really needed someone." I responded.

Then there is another, who treats me like family, a sister.

A friend of mine since the rough days of middle school.

Who has dealt with grief before,

An ally, she stares at me with concern.

Yes, a dear friend of mine.

My family members shared my grievances.

The efforts they make to cheer me up with their waves of laughter.

Keeping his memory alive in the house when it feels empty.

Thank you all for being there.

Mirror Mirror Where is She?

Her eyes once shiny,

Youthful,

Innocent,

Brighter than the sun and as clear as water,

Now, it is muddy and dull.

Beneath them are circles

Darkened from the sleepless nights.

Her complexion is shadowed with greys and blues.

Her skin was dewy yet dry from all the tears,

Bringing in the color red to her face.

The complexion of an apple.

She slowly wipes them away and grabs the hairbrush.

Her long flowy hair was completely matted,

Cutaway like yesterday's grass as the season changes.

Her clothes draped around her like chains of a prisoner.

Shades that once were yellow and blues are now black and browns.

Making little to no effort at all.

A shadow slowly hovers over her,

A friend,

Or foe,

Maybe she'll never know.

With one last look upon the mirror,

She turns off the lights and allows her image to fade.

Down Below Sea Level

As the feeling sits,

Like the bottom of the ocean;

There are mysteries yet to be unraveled.

Do not be fooled for where there are small fish,

Clownfish,

Dolphins,

And starfish, are

Massive whales and sharks.

All seeking the way of life.

Predator and Prey.

10/15-10/30

Dear my sweet little angel,

Halloween was coming. I was only a click away from purchasing your long-awaited costume. "You have something left in your cart" a message would appear, a silent reminder of what could've been. You would've been a lovely pirate. You have always been a sassy little dog and I bet you still are. The way you wore your collar proudly and how you would flaunt the cameo sweater that you insisted on wearing during the winter. Your personality continues to shine in my memories. It's always bittersweet.

Then the day comes, Halloween day. My thoughts resurface, bringing me back to the pirate costume. I could picture it all now. You would just adore the outfit, embracing the eye patch of where your eye had gone missing, and chewing the hat into pieces. Out of everyone who had dressed up, you would've been the star of the show I can promise that.

A costume was anticipated and planned for so long. "Halloween was supposed to be full of treats without tricks." is what whispered in the back of my head. A one-eyed pirate that sailed past the seven seas and will not return.

With that, I walk through the door into my costume. Missing my little pirate. I pray that you have found treasure in the great sea.

The Reality of the Situation

There are no more "what ifs"

There is just "What now"

A life in Despair's Shoes

Despair is in her small room.

Her body is frail as it could be.

Having the doors locked and windows shut

Filled with darkness and deafening silence.

Stinky from the old clothes and mold left in her room.

She lies on her bed,

resting her head on the pillow...

Unable to move at all.

As she stares up blankly at the ceiling

Tears fall on her face one by one.

Despair's black hair is as dark as her lungs and bones.

Empty and motionless.

Like a black hole in outer space.

A face with lifeless eyes and a frown.

She looks like a zombie as she wanders around

Wearing her headphones

Blocking out everything around her.

While clutching the pillow for comfort.

Finally, she goes outside.

Despair is lost.

Abandoned in a desert with the blistering stars above.

Driving for miles and miles

Without any guidance to reach out to-

Nor a sense of direction.

She pauses in the middle of the road,

Letting her pockets hold her hands.

She stands there gazing at what seems to be nothing.

Feeling alone,

A silent but deadly scream escapes her blood-red lips.

Then,

She goes home all over again.

Although pain is for a moment,

That moment turns into a lifetime ever so easily.

Like a needle in the skin,

Engraving a tragedy like a tattoo.

The Mind is dangerous.

Holding a quill in hand,

For time is not a thing.

The Internal II

Pounds of gunk covered me from head to toe. It felt heavy, almost as if sandbags surrounded my body. For some odd reason, I did not panic. It made me feel safe in some sort of unsettling way. The black residue covered the room from the neck down. I felt faint from the suffocation, yet I did not fight it. I waited for more to cover my head, accepting the end but that was all. When my lungs gave up, I lost complete consciousness. In the darkness, there was a warm feeling inside of me, I curled like a child hugging myself as if there was an invisible pillow there. Around me felt like a cold blanket. For a while, I stayed like this, until it was time to wake up once again. I spent my days like this, maybe even months. Falling asleep and waking up, not knowing the difference. I didn't try to escape because I had gone too comfortable. Then one day, the black gunk had hardened all around me. Panic had set in, and I became fully aware of my predicament. "You can't stay like this anymore," a small voice in the back of my head says. It's always been there telling me over

and over, but I had chosen to ignore it. Now I listen.

Keeping

We keep ourselves alone

To collect our thoughts,

Feelings,

And fears.

Locking ourselves in closed rooms,

Blankets sticking to our skin,

Flesh and bones decaying.

When the door opens,'

It's easier to hide behind perfect porcelain teeth

And long sleeves,

—All in cue.

The Stage and I

Dancing with the wind

As the music carries me,

Igniting the flames that have once died.

Sparked with passion,

Leaping,

Running,

Jumping,

This holy sensation.

The crowd roars,

Demanding more.

They punch the air with whips in their hand,

And I the animal

Outside of the cage.

The light hits my eyes, commanding them to blink.

They toss their garbage everywhere and

I roar back.

They smile in satisfaction.

Ah yes, agitating a ticking time bomb.

This is what *they want.*

I huff and turn away.

When the curtains draw,

And the show ends,

I am left with shackles.

The Villain Who Breaks

Hands tied behind my back.

In an isolated room,

Glued to the seat of the chair.

My eyes covered,

Yet I refuse to quiver.

The door opens.

Without footsteps.

Instead,

A chuckle follows.

"Miss me dearie" he whispers into my ears.

I do not shake.

I do not tremble.

Hear me roar!

"I will not let you break me.

Not now.

Not ever.

Because what you came here to break,

It's already broken."

I smirk and laugh like a maniac.

Yes, a maniac.

Breathing, just breathing.

Take a breath

1

2

3

Release

1

2

3

Take a breath and think.

"Now repeat by yourself."

Anger

Anger is strong.

When one is weak.

Defenseless.

Because all they can do now is curse at the sky.

Slowly Losing

"You need to get up!"

A hand tugs once more.

~~I want to but I can't.~~

A sigh escapes and eyes close.

A feeling I cannot shake off.

What has already been done,

What already has been said.

—— ~~But no one will understand even if they tried.~~

Yet something always remains.

11/2

Dear my sweet little angel,

Today my thoughts scurried all over the place as I spent the day reflecting…

Truthfully, I never believed in the word love until I found a new definition. A common misconception that I foolishly believed in is that "love" was only about romance. I believed that love was only existent in fairytales that I used to read as a child when, it is not. There is love in friendships, families, and much more. When you came into my life, I felt unconditional love. You accepted me for who I am, flaws and all, which was all I ever wanted. In my eyes, you were never just a dog but rather a friend I can talk to and my forever family. Now that you are gone, I have learned too late that love comes in a spectrum. It terrifies me how much loss can lead to a spiral of new meanings and ways of thinking about life. It just hits you

right in the face and spreads all around.

In Control

Every puppet needs strings to move.

But what if those strings were to be cut?

Severed like a burnt contract.

No one can control the puppet.

And the puppet cannot move without strings.

We Keep What's Hidden Until We Can No Longer Hide It Anymore

Like a domino,

All it takes is one wrong move

For everything to go down.

Losing you was the catalyst

For so many emotions,

That has been held back for so long.

Memories

Memories

Memories

I scoff at them now.

Sadness leaks

And Anger burns.

Hurt turns into steam.

Cascading upon my face,

The fumes eradicate the mask.

Let loose of those emotions.

To be honest and open.

Winter: Bringer of Life

As fall turns into winter,

There is a sense of

Trust

And coldness

That no fire can extinguish.

Instead, it burns the longer it's there.

I breathe it in

Allowing shivers to pass by my spine,

Head to toe.

Winter may seem dead,

But like me, it's alive.

The frost reminds me I am human.

The numbness has taken me to another level of my skin.

It holds my hands to remind me of my fondest memories.

A steaming cup of hot chocolate,

Reminding me what it feels like to be warm.

Snow creating a winter wonderland,

Where I once felt free.

For snow to come there must be a storm.

Thus the icicles drip down water, nourishing the crispy weeds.

Slowly Sinking

Some days the tides are stronger,

And the salt starts to fill my lungs.

The rocks scrape my back.

I swim up

But something is keeping me down.

A hand grasping my foot.

Who could it be?

A siren?

A mermaid?

I sink once again.

This time I let her.

For it is the only thing she can do now.

Surge

I would live within my denial thinking that it was all a dream.

Often argue between what's reality and imaginary.

After a while, it became severely unhealthy.

I needed to come to terms with reality once and for all.

Emotionally, I was also a train wreck.

One emotion that surprised me the most was anger.

I was angry at everything.

Angry at the world,

angry at the circumstances,

And angry at myself.

Some may turn their sadness into anger as a way to put all their

emotions into one basket.

Or like with me, emotions that have been locked away for so long

begin to unravel.

It's a rollercoaster of its own.

The only way I saw myself handling all these emotions was through

seclusion, which was good and bad.

If I Could Fly

If I could fly,

I would go past the moon.

Farther than the stars.

Away from the planets.

Continue on galaxies.

Make one with constellations.

My wings beating against the air,

Until they give out.

Just to see you happy in heaven.

11/26

Dear my sweet little angel,

Today is Thanksgiving. A day where people are thankful for what we _have_ along with what we _had_. I am thankful to have met such a wonderful dog. I am thankful for the times you have sat by my side when I needed you the most. I am thankful for the ups and downs we had down the road. Most important of all, I am thankful to have found my first ever friend. The lights in your eyes were like smoke signals on a stranded island. Your smile is completely intoxicating. Everything about you is and always will be perfect in my eyes. Even in death, you had an impact on me. If I could turn back time, I would do it all again, meeting you regardless of the hurt in the end.

To whom have helped me and provided comfort,

My family, who provides what I need, and the friends who

become like a family.

Thank you.

Wishful thinking

I dream of a time where you're next to me like any ordinary day.

Running in the grass underneath the beaming skies.

Basking in the sunlight as it glimmers over your fur.

Sitting by the doors on the rainiest days,

Trying to capture all those raindrops.

Bundled in blankets to keep warm.

All of us together in one place.

Laughing and singing.

We toss a ball, and you would bolt to it.

Prance around the block as we take you on walks.

As if time never existed and the oblivion and bliss were still there.

Recollection

The past is never truly escapable.

It's the truth.

Photographs hold evidence of what has been done.

Videos documenting what is said.

No matter what is burned or buried, the human brain will bring it

forward one way or another.

No one can turn back time.

The only thing to do is to keep moving forward.

The past can be good and bad.

It reminds us of the lessons we've learned,

And the mistakes that have been made.

The dates of the calendar don't mean anything.

That is until something happens.

Whether it is a good day or a bad day.

We remember.

My Saving Grace is Gone

My sweet little angel
What am I to do,
When you're not here?

My sweet little angel
Who drove away all my demons—
When I was struggling to fight them all alone.

My sweet little angel
Who built me up when the world tore me down,
Even when I had no faith in myself.

My sweet little angel
Who taught me how to swim
When all I could do was drown.

Now my sweet little angel is back into the heavens
While I am here.
Fighting.
Struggling.
To keep those demons away.
Do not let the tides take me away.

Beautiful Flower

A single white rose

Quickly run red.

Stained by blood.

Withering away,

Blooming again.

Black.

12/3

Dear my sweet little angel,

It is already December. At this point everything begins to register and set in, I can no longer live within my refutations. At this moment I sit here on my computer glancing at what I need to do. I am so close to the finish line of my courses. Winter break is about to begin, and I have no clue of how I will spend it. Lately, the sounds of the wind and rain soothe me to sleep. Of course, my sleeping schedule is not the same as it once was.

Entering the stores I see that Halloween and Thanksgiving have been replaced with Christmas lights and decorations. In my eyes, they are beautiful as they glimmer and hold a sense of joy that I have been missing. Christmas is one of my most favorite holidays, there was something about Christmas that made food taste sweeter

than it is. I don't know how to feel about it now these

days with everything that is happening, all I know is that it

won't be the same.

Poor Little Girl

Poor little human. Don't be sad.

I am here.

I am everywhere.

Why do you weep?

I am right here.

No need to cry.

I see you struggle——

Hiding the fact that you too can be happy.

I am okay now.

I am safe.

I can run to my deepest desires in an endless pool of dreams.

I can fly freely with nothing to keep me down.

I can do what I like.

Free of pain.

You struggle to breathe,

You struggle to sleep.

But it is okay.

Why do you walk like a zombie,

When you can buzz like a bee.

Why do you scream like a banshee?

When you could sing like a bird.

Here, I stand right in front of you.

Staying by your side when you cannot sleep

Suffocated by the world.

Catching all your tears when your eyes turn into a faucet.

Cheering you on whenever you fall and sink

Deeper into a quicksand of thoughts.

I am here,

But you cannot see me.

> Poor little human,
>
> Please do not cry.

> I am here,
>
> I am everywhere.
>
> I will wait next to you
>
> Till the day you die.

The Effects of Corruption

She was too innocent in this world.

You were all that was left.

Holding it tight

And creating hope.

Kept her at bliss

Of the things that caused her harm.

Now you are gone.

Look at what the world did.

Poor girl.

All alone.

Her heart turned into ash.

Stuffed animals all on the floor.

A massacre of blankets and pillows.

Her eyes slicing through souls as quickly as the words shooting out
of her lips.

Something the grim reaper could no longer control.

Like a volcano, she has erupted,

Destroying everything that comes.

Screaming into the depths of the forest,
Yet no one can hear.
All deafened by the loudness.

Bewildered from it all,
At last, she stops.

But is it anger?
No.
It is from something *more*.

The Internal III

I sat there looking at the world from a swing. My legs are propelling me higher and higher. Down below the plants flourished with rays of sunlight and clean raindrops to bathe them. Rainbows cascade the sky like decorations. It looked more beautiful up here than it does from down there. Birds chirped beside me singing some songs. There was a sense of euphoria. It scared me. It was altogether too peaceful. I couldn't allow myself to be ignorant so instead of enjoying the peace, I waited anxiously. I ruined it. Ruined my paradise. The ground shakes and throws me off the swing. I close my eyes, slipping into the air as if I were in a coma. I am falling.

Only You Could

You found the best parts of me

I didn't know existed.

Humanity and Toxicity

Why as a society do we not listen

Or see the signs of struggles when the red flags are held high.

Making sadness a competition.

Filling a bowl of toxicity only to be measured by pride.

Judging others struggles,

When we should be lifting each other up.

Empowering each other.

Consoling each other.

Where has humanity gone?

Was it fed off to Greed?

Jealousy?

Anger?

Why does it turn into a lion's den when vulnerability takes place?

Preying on each other's weaknesses and using them against each

other

like a sword.

Making pain tolerance a competition, as if the prize to be won is

awe and acknowledgment.

All sadness and pain are valid.

No matter the extent, big or small.

We all are human, and we hurt.

The ability of vulnerability is not weakness but rather displaying

great strength.

Self-Destruction

No one was there.

Instead, she befriended her demons.

Because they never leave.

Their words slither into her ears.

Feeding of what appears to be ~~truths~~ lies.

"You don't need them," They whisper.

Removing their gloves,

They caress her hand like a child. Dressing up in costumes.

"She'll never know the difference" they giggle.

She is aware.

She knows it.

"This is not healthy," she tells herself.

"What was that?" They panic in fear of losing their toy.

"Oh, nothing." She sings.

12/25

Dear my sweet little angel,

Merry Christmas! Are you gnawing on a big bone that you always wanted, I hope so. I can proudly say that you have been a good boy this year. Santa Clause would be proud. Speaking of Santa and his presents. I had to fight the urge to buy you a present every time I passed by a store. So many what ifs played in my mind. Questions like:

Would've I have bought you a new sweater?

A new toy?

New treats?

Would I have been out and about like I am now if you were still here?

I try to brush them off.

"There's nothing much I can do now." I reason with myself. Instead, I look at what is around me. The skies where I am are cloudy. I searched for signs of you, but it is only in the night where it is visible to see. The Christmas lights cascade across houses, streets, and Christmas trees, something that you would've liked. The presents underneath the trees don't matter anymore, for you are the great gift life could give. You were the gift that kept giving throughout those years.

Life in Sadness

Being happy is one of the scariest moments,

~~It feels ever so temporary...~~

Because when I feel sad,

~~I am no longer pretending, and I can feel...~~

It reminds me that I am alive.

The Lesson You Taught Me

How does a heart continue to beat?
When it has been torn, ripped, and shredded into tiny pieces.
Filled with scars.
And dragged across a rocky pavement.

So many times I trusted the ones I love, yet they did not love me
back.
I wore my heart with me. It shined so brightly.

Suddenly that shine began to dull.
It disappears.

There comes a time where I forgave them for hurting me.
Believing that I deserved it.

For a while I stayed in a dark hole, I dug myself.
Afraid to come out.

When I did, history would only repeat itself.
They would stand with a knife in hand (one that I had given them
for protection).
I should've kept it instead. I think to myself now looking back.

I trusted them.

Weapon in hand when I hold out my heart.

So

I

Tossed

it.

"Lesson learned." I remind myself as I see it falling.

Deep down I know I was scared.

That is why I did it.

Scared of it happening again.

But not when I am with you, my angel.

You flew down and caught it.

Minutes before it touched the ground.

You taught me to love myself.

When all I could do was hate myself.

Because you taught me self-love, I realized I did nothing wrong.

You gave me that confidence.

Taught me the truth.

"I did not deserve this treatment," I mumble to myself now.

Yes, I will remember.

It didn't matter anymore what they would think.

All that matters is knowing that I had one person who loved me for me.

I will remember.

Thank you for teaching me that.

Continuing Beyond the Grave

It was never about losing you,

it was about finding a way to keep going,

when you were gone…

keeping a fire when the rain would pore,

singing a song without a melody.

It feels impossible.

What I feel can't be replaced.

Your absence is one I sense.

They do not listen when I explain.

Almost the same sensation as a phantom limb.

All of this is something they can never understand.

Six Feet Below

There's nothing I can do or change about it.

If I had the power to go back in time, it would be no use.

Nothing could've been prevented.

The past can tamper but the future will stay the same.

I still would've lost you,

No medication,

Surgeries,

Or medical services could heal the pain of what you had gone

through.

I can't bring you back,

And I wouldn't want to.

Who am I to disrupt your peace up in the heavens above?

I would never be able to forgive myself for my selfishness if I were

to.

It's a cruel reality every person has to face.

One that takes time to come to terms with and accept.

Family into Foe: It's My Turn To Leave.

When he was gone,

A message appeared on my phone.

A message from someone who I once knew.

Who I had once loved and cared for.

The same person who pushed me down when I lifted you.

I see that you have heard the news.

Had the audacity to reach out.

After everything.

All I can say now is...

Please don't come back into my life,

Not when you walked away when I was at my lowest.

When I needed you the most you abandoned me.

When knives covered my back,

You added one more to the collection.

When I had my guardian angel,

He was there to shield me from the war of your actions.

The way you twisted my arm with your words.

You hurt me.

There is no excuse.
For the way, you played with my emotions
And I believe that I was the problem.
~~I believed you.~~

My angel has flown away now. Up in the sky.
No one to defend me now.
So I will build up my walls higher.

I will no longer be the fool.

You cannot come back into my life.
Once a piece of paper is crumpled and ripped, it's no longer the
same.
No matter how much you try to repair our relationship.

So I grab my phone,
Re-read your message,
Acknowledging how you try to come back into my life,

Remembering the times when we were innocent. I shake my head—

For the last time.
Inhale.
Press the delete button.
And move on.

A chapter in my life I can finally close.
Spending time with those who truly care about me.

It Is Up to You

When the world has stripped you of all your

Defenses,

The only options are to pick yourself up or allow yourself to

crumble.

Go on and choose.

Win or lose.

Succeed or fail.

Sun or Rain.

Spring or Fall.

Red or Blue.

Slither like a snake or fly like a bird.

Right hand or left.

Water or Wind.

"Go on. You can do it!"

Let's Win This Battle and Win the War

We all have demons.

But not everyone is

wrestling on the ground with the devil.

Gambling with two cards.

Or on the brink of losing.

Remember to be kind to yourself and others.

Because you never know,

How the weight of your words may

Carry,

Or weigh them down.

Know that the angel in the sky is by your side.

Cheering for you to win the battle.

Show them what you are made of.

I believe in you.

1/1

Dear my sweet little angel,

Happy New Year! There are so many mixed emotions in the air. There is this realization of the future without you there, a feeling of anticipation of what comes yet. Time all of the sudden felt like it had gone too quickly, now that I have looked back. I can feel it in my bones, that things will not be the same. It sounds cheesy but it is the truth.

Ruins

It's loud and unbearable in a crowded room.
Sounds floating from one ear to another.
Lungs slowly collapse in space.

Through a hurricane, the tree stands,
Yet the leaves perish and are torn. Scattered like flies,
Twigs surrounding its counterparts,
Reaching for the trunk.

The wind can howl and shriek,
They may protest.
So, send them.

The seas continue to rise,

>> Eating,

>> Stealing,

>> Hungry for more.

But the mountains and hills will not crumble.
They *take.*
And make anew.

The fish will swim.

When the sound ends.

Trees can always grow.

The flowers reach the sky once again.

Until next time.

For who knows where everything will land.

And So She Snapped

There is a time,   **where enough is enough.**

A rock begins to break.

An adult cries the tears that the inner child was not able to do.

So quickly everything faded.

As the blues turn into greys and white into black.

All of the ink then begins to pour.

The mirror has finally shattered.

She is free but now *burning*.

Yield

I'd advise you to

Own your pain.

Do not let it own you.

Take the reins.

While you can.

The Day We Met

I sat there in my room,

Mindlessly writing in my journal.

Private thoughts that can never be unleashed.

I had asked my father for a dog.

That night I prayed until my lungs gave out.

I prayed for a friend.

It was all I ever wanted.

You were all I ever *needed.*

I was nervous not knowing what to expect.

There was no doubt you would like my family. People usually do.

"Would he or she like me?" I asked myself.

I heard a sound at the door.

My father came home from work.

When the door opened for some reason, I decided to sit on the
floor.

Instinctively I opened my arms.

None of it was planned yet my body and mind knew what to do.

A small fluff ball

With the biggest smile ran into my arms.

An instant connection.

A feeling I never experienced.

One I thought I would never feel.

I play that day every day in my head.

Holding a picture of you in my hand,

I bite back the flood in my eyes.

All I can ever say is "I miss you. My first ever friend. My best

friend."

Changes Without You

I am at a point where so much has changed in such a little time.

I always knew I would graduate, but never thought I would do it

without you.

I always knew that I was going to get these braces removed but I

had never suspected you were not able to see the new set of teeth.

I always thought that I would need to stay home to watch over you,

But now, all I see is a reason to leave.

All these changes are bittersweet because I always imagined you

there.

Celebrating my successes.

Seeing my progress.

Standing with my family at my graduation.

Celebrating my transfer.

Both of us growing old beautifully.

In my eyes, you were always like a puppy.

Motivated me when I woke up in the morning.

Running outside until our feet tire out.

You were my rock to hold me,

And I, the paper who was blown away by the whispers of the wind.

The anchor to the ship called "Life" when I felt the tides swaying

me all around.

Now, I must do it all,

With you in spirit.

How the Tables Have Turned

From my experience and those, I have talked with,

I think we can all agree that one of the most difficult things is

making those big choices.

In this context, I am referring to the choices that are associated

with the passing of a loved one. The first hello is as memorable and

intense as the last goodbye.

There would be times where I had blamed myself for making such

a decision.

I remember the days when I was younger and naïve,

I would think to myself, "I would never make a decision like that".

Now, I completely understand why.

It felt awful but necessary, for I wouldn't want him to live in pain.

I saw how much my little angel had suffered and I would not want

him to worsen.

Forgiving myself will always be very difficult.

Where are you now?

I can't help but question,

Are you up in the heavens living your best life?

Are sitting on the clouds watching me go through life?

Are you still out there, somewhere in the great beyond waiting for

me?

I feel you in my heart,

But lost all sense of physicality.

Pieces of you linger but I cannot tell if it is a figment of my

imagination or reality.

Are you running around an endless field feeling free as the wind

itself?

Traveling as you please.

Can you hear me when I talk to the walls when no one else is

around?

Listening to every word and understanding it all.

In my saddest moments are you there sitting beside me? Or is it

just me?

Possibilities run through my head, as I imagine you in every new

memory I make.

Almost as if you're there. Yet again, scenarios and "what ifs" may

blind my judgment and change my emotions.

What could've been happy, turns bitter within each thought.

"Just be happy, enjoy life human. Don't worry about me." I can

almost hear you tell me.

Have you moved on to the next life?

Reincarnated as someone or something I have passed by.

If so, I pray that you are happy and healthy. I pray that we meet

again whether it is through the gates of heaven, past the rainbow

bridge, or in the next life.

All I know is that I need to see you again, at least one more time.

Even if it is from a distance, you being happy and at peace is all I

ever need.

1/16

Dear my little angel,

Many people may ask me "Why do you write those letters?" They may respond with things such as "He's a dog he can't and will never read, see, or understand them" and while they gawk, I continue to write.

To those people, my response is "I write to him for many reasons, reasons that you may not understand, hence why you ask such a question."

Resurface

There was a time where I had become worried about myself.

Concerned that I have fallen too far into the deep end.

Unsure if I'll resurface once again.

It became ever so unsettling.

Almost as if I had lost myself,

In an endless sea.

A small child, with a big fishnet

Was looking for me.

It took a while, but she did find me,

Or more so,

I found her.

It was bittersweet.

Past It All

The past is never truly escapable.

It's the truth.

Photographs hold evidence of what has been done.

Videos documenting what is said.

No matter what is burned or buried, the human brain will bring it

forward one way or another.

No one can turn back time.

No one can change what we've done.

The only thing to do is to keep moving forward.

The past can be good and bad. Please remember that.

It reminds us of the lessons we've learned,

And the mistakes that have been made.

Like yin and yang, we need both.

The dates of the calendar don't mean anything.

That is until something happens.

Something unforgettable such as a birthday,

Anniversary,

Or a day of passing.

Whether it is a good day or a bad day.

We remember.

Working without an Anchor

With grief, you never know what to expect.

Unlike a recipe, there is no instruction or consistency.

It brings out the worst of the worst.

Unlocking a pandora box with one touch.

The emotional and mental turmoil.

It's a constant battle where some days are calmer than others.

Mini battles that are manageable.

Easy,

And laughable.

Those are the good days.

Then the war strikes. Everything comes crashing down.

Those are the bad days,

the days that leave a pain in the chest.

Once again, unexpectedly.

Sometimes incomprehensible and difficult to describe.

Coming in different shapes and forms.

Each has its trigger.

It feels like learning to steer a ship for the first time.

Listening for signs of land in the middle of the sea.

Steering with great might every time the shore shifts.

Wondering if a storm is coming and if the ship will make it.

We Are Human

I'll be honest,

Some days are going to be hard.

So hard that you will feel like all of your oxygen is sucked out of

your lungs, and your heart feels like it could no longer beat.

Losing the ones we love can make us feel empty.

Alone.

Abandoned in this big world.

The sensation of walking into a bear trap.

Hurting the more we try to escape.

Self-control and awareness will be one of the few things that will

help

To get out of your head.

Telling yourself the gravity of the situation.

There will be days where you wonder what you are fighting for.

And that is okay.

It is called being human.

We feel.

On the days we don't feel,

You ARE feeling.

I will not lie. Times get tough. Dark.

But I promise you, it will be worth the fight.

Nothing is better than that feeling of reaching the top of the

mountain.

The feeling of overcoming.

The feeling of believing in yourself.

Remember those feelings. The best ones.

Keep doing what makes you feel that certain way.

For we only live once, might as well make it last.

The "Why"

Most of the time we wonder why things happen.

And more often, we may never get an answer.

Sometimes we need to search for the answer, for it will not fall

to our laps.

As a firm believer of "things happen for a reason",

I simply wait until a reason surfaces somehow and somewhere.

Dismay and Recovery

So much fear stems from loss.

It's the fear of losing someone again.

The fear of starting again.

The fear of being hurt.

So many qualities and pieces are missing. For they are with the

people who took a piece with

them to heaven.

The Internal IV

I sat there holding your picture in front of my eyes. It was of you laying down very sleepily. I touched it with the tip of my fingertip remembering how things were. A small memory plays. Everything transforms around me into what is my backyard. I stood there and I watched my younger self playing with you. I giggled each time you licked the palm of my hands and cheered every time you did a trick. We played several rounds of fetch until the sun started to set. From my present point of view, I took a step closer to see myself. My hair was much longer and there was more youthfulness. How different we looked now. I looked down and there you were right beside her sleeping like a baby. Looking angelic as possible. I held in a laugh as I heard you snoring like a troll. Something I did not expect. I leaned down to stroke your fur but like a ghost, my fingers brushed through you. A sigh escaped my lips. Now in the present time, I opened the curtains

letting in light for once, and always kept that photo beside me.

Until We Meet Again

While you're gone,

I'll be missing you.

Holding on to the collar you once wore.

The only thing I have left of you.

I'll keep my memories of you alive.

Like the times you made me laugh,

Or the times you've surprised me by your acts of kindness.

I refuse to forget you.

I'll remember all of the times your eye lit up

Like a firefly in a forest.

So gentle and ecstatic.

Living like how you wish you wanted me to.

Basking in opportunities.

Taking chances.

Not letting my demons get the best of me.

While you wait in the heavens,

I'll stay true.

Live without regrets.

Live life as if I was living for two souls.

Forever and always.

I love you.

Grief

The thing with grieving is that so many people make it out as

something that you can move on from.

When in reality it is something that you will forever feel.

You feel it when you come across an old picture of them.

You feel it when you hear their favorite song on the radio.

You feel it in the back of your mind, as it slowly tries to inch its

way to the surface.

Grieving never truly ends.

A person can go on for years being happy. They may live the life

they ever so desire.

But at the end of the day,

We can never truly move on with the fact that the person is no

longer here.

Their absence is the elephant in the room you cannot ignore.

We continue to miss them.

We remember their birthdays,

The way they looked,

Their favorite foods,

The smallest details about them,

and

How they passed.

We all still feel a sense of grief without realizing it.

1/22

Dear my little angel,

It still dawns on me now and then that a new year has begun. A whole new chapter is being opened and there is nothing I can do but follow the script of this life. I felt so much from the start that I didn't know what to do with these emotions. The only thing I could do is to write with a pencil in hand to filter a small increment of what was happening inside. I felt alone in it all. I search for songs, books, and just about anything to see if anyone felt the same way. It wasn't until I compiled these letters and poems is when I realized I am the answer. I hope that this will allow others to make them feel less alone like how you made me feel. You always were the one to make bad things good and so I will do the same.

One thing that will stay constant in this life and cannot be

explained in simple words is how much I miss you. I will

never forget you and everything you do. I will still write to

you as if I am updating you on my life and quietly

celebrate holidays by imagining you by my side.

Know that I love you so much. I will think of you

always for this is not the end.

Love, Alexa.

Made in the USA
Las Vegas, NV
23 July 2022

52064836R00088